ISBN-13: 978-1533045102

ISBN-10: 1533045100

To: (Cameron) Cam Bam
There is so much amazement
that comes with knowing you.
Thank you for all the wonderful
memories.

OPEN THE DOOR PLEASE?

~Celeste Ennis Bicknell~

Learning Lee

1

Lee had his own ways of doing things. That's for sure. He would look at you as if he wasn't really listening. The whole time you wondered if he was hearing you perfectly or if he really couldn't hear you, in that moment. He stared off into space and when he did, he seemed to be lost in his own little world. Abby knew from the time he was almost 3, that he was uniquely made. He was different in the most spectacular ways. She knew he was a puzzle that many would have a hard time solving or understanding. She just knew. Nothing came easy with Lee.

He created a challenge, with everything he did. He was such a busy one. He demanded so much time and energy, but he was such a lovely little boy. You just had to learn Lee.

Abby, felt she had few minutes to herself. She got so frustrated quite often, and for that, she felt guilty. Lee's hypnotic blue eyes and charismatic smile, helped to ease her level of frustration on most days though. He warmed her heart and before she knew it, she was smiling right along with him.

Boys Will Be Boys

2

Abby devoted, what seemed like, every minute, to keeping Lee out of mischief. Every day was like an adventure. Each day was unlike the day before. You just never knew what his next move would be.

When he began to flap his little arms in excitement, it meant something was about to happen. It meant get ready for anything. The faster he waved his arms, the quicker you had to be ready... If he could have taken flight, he would've. Just before his next move, you could see the buildup of excitement in intensity of his hands. He was filled with curiosity and wanted to touch everything in his path.

When the excitement could no longer be contained, he grabbed you close and hugged you tightly. He gave the best hugs. They were deliberate and so heartfelt. When you heard him shrill, you knew he was thrilled at what would be his next move,

and it was going to be anything

but ordinary.

"His Way"

3

He had noticeable quirks.
It was just the Lee way. Things
had to be done just so. He
didn't want his food to touch,
pushing the bacon from the
path of the eggs or at lunch,
the peas away from his mashed
potatoes. He was adamant

about that. "NO touching!" He would say.

If he kept his shoes on it was a miracle. He could not stand to have them on. He loved the feel of the carpet or the grass beneath him. Where fireworks or the revving of a motorcycle's engine were too loud for some, they weren't too loud for him. He gravitated to the noise. He yelled at the top of his lungs when he saw or heard a motorcycle, "BICYCLE!" It gave him so much joy. The noise seemed to sooth him. It was his happy place.

He would often hum just as loudly. He'd hum when he was happy or when he was sleepy or when he was eating.

Humming was Lee's thing.

There was always a song to be sung and sometimes only he knew the words. It was a song that was so memorable and so enjoyable, that Lee just had to move and sway to the beat. He marched to the beat of his own tune. He was the conductor of the most wonderful sounds. He would

hum and not long after, you

were humming too. He was a

happy child.

Open the Door Please?

4

He darted for the front door, to make his way to the street, more times than Abby and Brian could count. Brian was less worried about Lee leaving out the door, than Abby was. Brian created a way to keep him from being able to just run out the front door. All the doors had a special knob on them, that Lee hadn't mastered yet. But, when the door was slightly ajar or when he was already outside, he'd run at top speed. It irritated Abby but she tried not to let on.

The moment she let her guard down, or tried to relax,

was the moment he took off again. He flashed that huge smile and away he ran. He was so fast. Abby had a hard time keeping up with him.

You could count on Lee to do many things routinely. He would repeat himself in cycles of three and he absolutely, positively, without reserve, loved opening and closing doors .... And he never met a door that he didn't like. He would open and close his car door before the engine started. He would open and close the mailbox. He would open and close his bedroom door and the microwave too. Doors were a Lee thing and he loved doing it.

He began to run across the street, to her home, but Abby held his hand firmly. Brian glanced from what he was doing, which was usually household chores, and smiled. He saw Lee running hurriedly toward her.

Lee threw his arms around IssaBella. She was one of his favorite people. He half sang and half said her name while he rocked her to and fro. "Is-sa-bel-la! Is-sa-bel-la! Is-sa-bel-la! Come on. Puter please!" Lee said. He saw a cell phone nearby and equated it with his own device. Abby bought him a Kindle to help keep calm and she hoped it would help with his hand-eye coordination.

IssaBella headed toward the opened garage door, but not before Lee cut her off at the path. He asked his infamous question. "Open the door please?" He reached out in anticipation for the door. Open the door please? Open the door please? Open the door please? He couldn't wait a second longer for her approval. He opened the door and closed it before IssaBella could respond. They both laugh and shared a hug. She knew his routine and simply learned to wait patiently for him to complete his last open-close pattern before entering her home. After all, they were the best of friends.

Dance Party!!!

The sound of the radio was playing and Lee started swaying back and forth. He loved music. It didn't matter the tune, Lee was going to move to the beat. He participated in a kind of rocking motion that was always in sync with the beat. Not long after he started, he would yell, "Dance Party!" That was his way of letting everyone around him know to join in. The fun was about to begin. He loved being around IssaBella and her siblings. They partied if he wanted and never complained.

Lee was an only child. He really got to experience a big family with IssaBella and her many brothers. They were all

his family too. They treated

him as if he was their youngest

sibling. Being around them

was like having a birthday

party every day and he was

happy with a party anytime he

could get one.

Uniquely Lee

6

A day in the life of Lee is anything but boring. His quirks help to make him who he is. He isn't difficult or purposely trying to push buttons. He is passionate about what he likes, what he doesn't, what he wants, and what he needs. He just has a very specific way of doing things. He is a piece to a puzzle that requires more time and effort. He requires you really getting to know him and opening your mind to his differences.

Yes, he happens to be autistic, but more importantly, he is uniquely Lee.

THE END

On to the next adventure…

The only way I have truly known to be me, is through self- expression. I have found that what noise I create, is often the voice for others, who dare not make a sound."

~Celeste Ennis Bicknell~

www.ingramcontent.com/pod-product-compliance
Lightning Source LLC
Chambersburg PA
CBHW050838290526
45792CB00001B/439